Memories of Nortl

Our latest booklet deals with the are   r.
North End is probably a shortened versio   n
road from what is now Old Portsmouth ɪ   d
Kingston at Kingston Cross where the ᴛᴡᴏ ᴊᴏᴀᴅ   ·d
along what is now Old London Road then Peronne Road and over the creeк to Cosham. When the roads were re-aligned Portsbridge replaced the old bridge and London Road was straightened. There were one or two large houses along the route north which will be mentioned in the location where they formerly stood.

Stubbington Farm occupied most of the area and dates back many years. Until the Dissolution of the Monasteries it was owned by Southwick Priory. Stubbington was conferred as a dower of Anne of Cleves, subsequently passed to Katherine Howard and, after her death, was exchanged by Henry VIII for land of Winchester, St Marys College in July 1543. Various tenant farmers occupied it over the years. Later the college sold off some land to the Ridge family and the Thistlethwaytes. From 1788 to 1815 Thomas Thistlethwayte of Southwick, leased it to Thomas Fitzherbert who lived in Stubbington Lodge. In 1901 the farm was sold and the pond drained (the pond site was the east side of Balfour Road, between Laburnum Grove and Stubbington Avenue). The farmhouse stood more or less where the Ascension Church is now.

"I remember North End from my childhood. The main area at the crossroads seemed so busy. There was Whites, Melanies, Empress Ballroom on top of the Empress Garage. Across the road was the Chocolate King with Seals, Harris the funeral directors, public toilets and bus sheds. In between Gladys Avenue and London Road was the prominent Southdown Offices. They told you about green buses which took you into the country. The City buses were red. At one time there was a bus service from Stubbington Avenue to the Good Companion passing Baffins Pond. It was a single decker so people referred to it as a 'Little Bus'. Most buses were double deckers then. I used the 'Little Bus' quite often to visit the Odeon and Regent Cinemas. The Odeon was a very comfortable cinema in a certain style. The Regent Cinema was the other side of London Road but in another style. Its main distinction was a promenade around the side of the circular auditorium. You could look over the audience for your friends. Sadly this grand cinema was sacrificed for a supermarket. There was a Boots Chemist near Kingston Crescent, opposite Chichester Road. They had the unusual fashion of a lending library. After a while you could buy the books with a green shield on the front."

Anton Cox

"What a lovely place North End was when I was a youngster. From the Green Posts to Kingston Cross, a collection of shops – drapers, milliners, clothing etc. There was Belmonts a high class dress and coat shop, always a beautiful selection of clothes, which were one offs, and didn't cost the earth. At North End itself was the tram station and behind the corner of Stubbington Avenue was their Social Club. My husband and I used to go to play whist there and there were always 60 tables or more. Carrying on down where Safeways (since becoming Somerfield) now is was the Regent Cinema and then Marks & Spencer. The other side of the road was Bulpitts a drapery store who sold everything to do with dressmaking. There were banks, food stores and the like with an amazing array of goods. Of course in those days, 1920-1930, women had to go out every day for fresh meat etc. for that days dinner, no frozen goods. One last thing I mustn't forget the churches, St. Marks on the corner of Derby Road, then further down London Road Baptist."

Dorothy Aslett

"My first association with London Road began in 1938 when I was sixteen years of age and we moved into 50 Stirling Street. Previously we had lived at 13 Wells Street, Landport - a stones throw from Commercial Road and Charlotte Street with their great variety of large stores. We soon found London Road had its mix of many large and small shops and was able to satisfy all our needs satisfactorily most times. It offered a more personal and competitive service without the need to travel to Commercial Road. The six of us - Mum, Dad and four boys - soon appreciated our new environment. Three of us were working and the youngest was still at school and for the first time we were living in a house with a bathroom - to us a luxurious improvement in our way of life at Wells Street. London Road for us started on the corner of Kingston Crescent with Burtons the tailors where you could buy a tailor-made suit for two pounds ten shillings. In those days that was a lot of money for the basic wage was only two pounds twelve shillings a week, but it was every young man's ambition to be well dressed. I only purchased one suit from there and that was about 1943 - a beautiful blue all wool suit and that was a sales offer with a special clothing coupon arrangement. Sadly that shop has long gone, you now get your suits off the peg, made abroad and compared to what you got at Montague Burtons inferior in quality, cut and style. Next door was a small tobacconists, Osbornes. This was a very special establishment where customers could have tobacco made up to suit their to individual palates and the aromas from their specialist pipe mix. There was no need to go any further every thing you ever needed was here provided you could afford it. The exception being a pawnshop but there was one of these in Kingston Road which ended at the junction of Kingston Crescent where London Road started. The number of grocers, butchers with other retail businesses mostly branches of national chains. One shop myself and many others frequented was the Chocolate King on the corner of Angerstein Road, to me a constant temptation which often led me to buy their broken nut milk chocolate which I would greedily eat and enjoy as soon I had bought it often leaving me with a badly upset stomach often resulting in sickness! On one Sunday my wife to be and I went to Gosport to visit my Uncle Arch Clark by the ferry. I made the mistake of gorging a bag of broken nut chocolate. Coming back the crossing was rough and I was disgustingly sick. An incident which taught me a severe lesson and my weakness cured, for my fiancee made clear to me she was not impressed by this incident and was not to be tolerated. My visits to Mr. Garcia, the Chocolate King, ceased but our relationship while it lasted had been enjoyable and I still enjoy chocolate but in moderation. On the eastern side of London Rd. opposite Kingston Crescent stands what's left of the Blue Anchor, a now one storey public house which before it became a victim of Portsmouth's first bombing raid in 1940 was a two storey building which at one time belonged to our family. I well remember this raid for we were sitting around the dinner table eating our meal when the sirens sounded. Our father led us into Stirling Street and we watched the bomber flyover and then we heard the bombs exploding. Dad went into the house and came out with his tin hat on and his gas mask slung over his shoulder pushing his cycle towards Kingston and London Roads where you could see a huge cloud of dust and debris rising. We followed and saw shop windows shattered, the Library and Police Station badly damaged. As I stood watching a Corporation lorry arrived with rescue workers from Central Depot to clear the road, my Dad was organising the sweepers from Powerscourt Road depot (where he was foreman) to knock the glass that remained in the shattered shop windows out. A lorry driver came over to me saying 'Frank you may be needed at Drayton Road School where Harry Austin is with a van' (Harry being a work mate of mine at Central Depot garage). So I walked round to the school to find Harry being helped to load a pine coffin into a van. The coffin contained the remains of Sid Flux - a popular boxer and had become the first person to die through enemy action in Portsmouth and was engaged to a girl who was the daughter of a neighbour in Wells Street, Landport. Further along this side of the London Road there were a variety of shopping opportunities that would put many modern shopping precincts to shame. On the northern side of Stubbington Ave. was Melanies dress shop with the Empress Ballroom on the first floor. During the war, despite the bombing the ballroom was the meeting place for the local teenagers once a week. When a raid took place everybody had to leave the hall but were allowed to return after the all clear sounded. This was one of the few places where you could meet your friends in comfort with good music for a small admission fee. I remember one night the sirens sounded my friend Fred Pullen and I had to leave the dance hall and so we went to the Clarence Gardens and bought ourselves a drink but the raid got so bad that the Landlord shouted 'everybody out and you can take your beer into our Air Raid Shelter'. However, to get into it you had to step down onto a tea- chest and unfortunately for me I might have been a little too enthusiastic in jumping down onto this chest when it collapsed under me sending beer everywhere, which did not please those who were drenched and leaving myself shocked, suffering a badly grazed leg and torn trouser leg. Another occasion in the 1960's when the Portsea Island Co-operative Society had purchased the premises, my Trade Union branch decided it would hold a social evening with a Buffet Dance at the Empress. As the vice-chairman I was given the task of seeing that it was an enjoyable evening. Together with members of the branch executive to assist and act as stewards, the Chairman of the Cleansing and Haulage Dept. along with the manager were invited as guests and we held our first Annual Branch Social. The annual dinner and dance still takes place today where members can bring their wives and enjoy themselves. Further along at 302 London Road was Ms. Joan Stonehams, Rathgar Hall, School of Dancing where my friend Fred Pullen and I decided we would enrol, pay our two shillings and six pence a week and become reasonable dancers! The sessions were very well organised and enjoyable. Most of the students were young women and Ms. Stoneham a good teacher who maintained strict discipline whilst teaching until one Wednesday night Fred and I decided during the half time break to adjourn to the Green Posts - public house opposite to enjoy a beer but on our returning Joan Stoneham asked Fred to dance with her and smelt the beer immediately. She told him that she would not allow anyone who had been drinking to dance with her young lady students and so our dancing lesson: ceased abruptly and we regretted having that beer for we had enjoyed our evenings at Ms. Stonehams school of dancing."

Frank Deacon

The following lists are based on the 1960 Kellys Trade Directory

Balfour Road named after the Lord Balfour, former Prime Minister. Residential only although earlier number 47 had been a grocers shop.

Battenburg Avenue, named after the Battenberg family, the spelling has always been incorrect.

South Side
here are Randolph and Kensington Roads
        J. & N. Wade, Electrical Factors

North Side
1a   Pankhurst (Weymouth) Ltd. Motor Cycle Agents

here are Randolph Road and Kearsney Avenue
        St. Nicholas Church
        The church was originally planned to have been St. Chad's in St. Chad's Avenue. It was built as a mission church to St. Marks in 1928 to seat 250 at a cost of £6,000. The architect was A. E. Cogswell.

Beaulieu Road, named after the Lord or village. Residential only
Belgravia Road, named after the district of London.

"I was on a party telephone line with number 40, but this was no bother about any nosiness as far as I know, these days this situation would spell trouble. There was no gas installed apart from gas fired central heating, although there were still traces of the old gas mantles. I used up the coal that had been left behind on the front grate the first winter we lived there. The first winter we lived there, there was a burst pipe, I couldn't remember where to turn the water off. I knocked one side and he didn't bother to listen to me being more concerned with his daughter saying goodbye to her boyfriend. The other side, Miss Goodenough helped, we managed to snap the top off of the inside tap and couldn't manage the outside tap. At last the water company showed up, water was pouring through the middle bedroom into the downstairs hallway by now. Eventually the ceiling fell down, a year later the kitchen ceiling fell down, so we had to have three ceilings repaired, replastered and artexed. One of the friends of the family managed to repair the pipe quickly and helped us with the insurance claim."

Sylvia Webb

Beresford Road named after the Admiral Residential only, although pre-war there had been a small shop at number 45.

Burlington Road, named after the Lord or district of London. East Side
56   Mrs. Bessie Jones, Corsetiere

Chelmsford Road, named after the Essex town.
East Side
38   H. G. Hayes, Motor Cycle Repairers
42   W. & S. Rabbitts, Grocers

West Side
7   Edward Butler, Decorator
41   Sydney Jones, Teacher of Music

here is Kirby Road
51   Frederick Coley, Teacher of Music He was one of the organists at
            St. Mary's Church.

Chichester Road named after the Sussex city.
South Side
6   Cox & Loader, Confectioner Now a shop selling sweets and
            groceries from Poland, Estonia and similar countries.

10   F. Treloggan, Ladies' Hairdresser Still a hairdresser in 2005.

"They had an excellent reputation, Mrs. Fisher was the lady in charge and all her staff were always very busy. In those days there was a three year apprenticeship and two years improving. I remember her always making sure the mirrors and floors were perfect."

Margaret Webster

12-14   Southcott's Builders

"This was a general hardware shop selling wood, glass, paint, screws & nails, tools and everything that you now go to large out of town type stores for. The main shop was on the left with large items stored at the back. On the right were two large areas where sheets of wood and glass could be cut to size."

Stephen Pomeroy

here is Havant Road

34	Hospital Savings Association Later a typewriter sales centre and now a Doctors.
54	Illuminations (W. J. Dowling) Electrical Contractors here is Emsworth Road
56	Mrs. Margaret Savidge, Shopkeeper Grocers and greengrocers, later run by the Wassell family.
66	Arthur Folland, Hairdresser Later was a hardware and then a florists.
76	G. T. Bedford, Fried Fish Shop Operated as a Fish and Chip shop for many years, is now a Chinese Takeaway.

here is Drayton Road

7	Pelham Hotel, Ernest Parkman Built in 1887 to designs of architect A. E. Cogswell, it has been known as the Pelham Hotel or Pelham Arms. It was originally a Pike Spicer brewery house. It was named after Lord Chichester whose family name was Pelham.
110	B. A. Marsh, Hairdresser Mr. Marsh continued here, cutting hair in his eighties, even after recovering from a stroke.
128	Mrs. E. Birrell, Confectioner
176	Cawtes Express Valet Service, Dyers & Cleaners
178	John Healey, Butcher Still a butchers shop in 2005.
180	V. E. Chase, Stationer and Post Office. Here is Farlington Road
182	Lord Chichester, Edwin Thompson Built in 1906 or 1909 depending which books you believe. It was a Brickwoods brewery house.

"Peter Lee used to be landlord of the Lord Chichester in the late sixties, early seventies, he had a boxer dog called Simba. Beryl his wife was having a chat with a good old boy about life after death, and he said when I die I'll give you a sign a bird will fly into the bar, he died and the bird flew in, make what you like of this."

Sylvia Webb

184   Brunswick Family Laundry Co. Ltd., Receiving Office. When the laundry closed Portsmouth Stamp shop moved here from London Road where they had been at Vernon Court.

"In 1988 we were between printers so Jeff Coast and the Portsmouth Stamp Shop hold memories of hard work and satisfaction. Our WEA Local History books were in great demand. Jeff would photocopy and we would collect the sheets in a shopping trolley, lay all the pages out on the floor of a members lounge, collect pages into booklets, staple and fold the booklets. In that year 3,650 were produced and 3606 sold by Blackwells, the Central Library and Porters. This was in the days when we sold books from 20p to 50p."

Margaret Webster

186   John Smith, Boot Repairer
192   Leslie White, Grocer
194   A. J. Ware & Sons, Greengrocers. Still trading as Wares in 2005, the main trade is wholesale selling prepared vegetables to hotels, public houses and restaurants.
196   J. Humphreys, Fishmonger. Later a bakery for a few years.

here is Paulsgrove Road
202   C. Smith, Hairdresser. Still a hairdresser in 2005.

here is Preston Road
214   Percy Lintott, Confectioner
230   W. Morris, Household Appliances here is Bedhampton Road
232   H. W. Russell & Son, Fried Fish Shop
236   Kenneth Beauchamp, Newsagent
1   Dittman & Malpas Ltd., Corn Merchants. The shop was purchased and demolished to allow Ashling Lane, the service road at the rear of London Road to be built.

"In the front they sold loose and packeted food for animals, birds, rabbits etc. They sold Canaries and other small birds as well and these could be seen in the rear room."

Stephen Pomeroy

3   William Braiden, Watchmaker
15   William Marsh, Plumber, House Decorator and Electrician

here is Havant Road

17	Stanley Milner, Watchmaker
39	Frederick Kissick, Greengrocer

"He sold from an electric van while his wife worked in the shop"

here is Emsworth Road

41	J. Campbell, Shopkeeper

"Stokes newsagent was here, now it is a hairdresser called Foxy Lady."

Sylvia Webb

59a-61	H. T. Peace, Grocer

here is Drayton Road

65	Frederick Hawkins, Butcher
77	Harry Sarch, Tailor
79	E. & A. Patrick, Wireless Engineers

"Mrs Patrick ran the shop while her husband worked for the Admiralty on the hill. Mr Patrick repaired radios and other appliances. They sold light bulbs, batteries, electrical fittings and small appliances. When they retired to Warsash the shop was sold and converted into a house."

Stephen Pomeroy

here is Beresford Road

83   Arthur Reeves, Chiropodist Later Matthews, husband and wife
          practised here.

"The Matthews were originally from Scotland, Mr. Matthews was quite a character, he had a boat in his garden that he had been working on for years. When he retired due to ill-health, Mrs Matthews continued to practice. They were both extremely good."

Margaret Webster

99   North End Carriers (Frederick Humphreys), Furniture Removers

here are Balfour and Beaulieu Roads

121-123   Portsea Island Mutual Co-operative Society Ltd., Grocers. Now a
          One-Stop shop and Post Office, 2005
127   H. Waldron & Son, Hardware Stores
129   Cyril Hayter, Greengrocer
133   Ascension Hall Listed in 1908 as the Ascension Sunday School. In
          1910 it was used as a church but reverted to being the church hall.
          It was used until 1968 when it was sold to the Seventh Day
          Adventists. They have since re-roofed and renovated the front of
          the church.
137   Mrs. H. Calver, Grocer

here is Burlington Road

153a   W. Morris, Jeweller
155a   W. Morris, China & Glass Dealer. Later all the Morris shops came
          together in Copnor Road

here is Farlington Road

169   Harold Voysey, Fried Fish Shop

"Known as the Bay Window since it had no shop front as such but had the queue in the front room and the fryer in the middle room. It was very popular in the area."

Stephen Pomeroy

171   Harry Turner, Draper
173   John Wright, Butchers
177   Rosella, Confectioner "Piccadilly sweet shop"
181   Silver Grey Line Taxis, A. Abbott
185   Mrs. Richards, Grocer
187   Hy. Eccles, Confectioner

here is Lyndhurst Road

189	D. & A. Stores, Grocers here is Paddington Road
213	E. L. Savidge, Grocers. Still a corner shop grocers in 2005.
233	George Burnett, Builder & Decorator.
	This was also a shop selling DIY materials and later became a video shop before being converted into flats called Craig House.

here are Belgravia and Kensington Roads

255	Mrs. H. Booth, Grocers
279	Miss Grace Fox, Teacher of Music

Compton Road
South Side

2	Albert Saunders, Decorator St. Nicholas Church Hall
90a	Rev. R. Eckersley

Copythorn Road named after the village.
South Side

20-24	Copythorn Road Garage. Late Little Wonder Coaches (P. W. Lambert, Petersfield) from 1948 to 1953. Still in use as a car repair garage in 2005.
52	Frederick Glenister, Fruiterer

"He used to deliver door to door from his electric van."

here is Kensington Road
Crofton Road
East Side

North End Secondary Modern School for Girls, motto "Be Thou Diligent"

"My memories of Lyndhurst Road Girls School are mostly happy. I attended there in the fifties when I was eleven and left at fifteen. Each day I walked from Buckland with my friend, we both went home for lunch. The time walking was spent learning our homework. The winters were much colder with icy pavements and snow hanging from the gutters. There were some excellent teachers who you admired and had respect for, but also teachers who were unable to control the class. My favourite lessons were English, history, geography and religion, my least favourites were P.E. music and maths. In 1954 the headmistress was Miss H. M. Leighton, class mistress M. E. Vine with 40 in a class."

Margaret Webster, nee King

here is Kirby Road
Domum Road Residential only.

Drayton Road, named after the nearby village
East Side
14   S. Holden, Shopkeeper

here is Wymering Road
            North End Secondary Modern School for Boys. Now part of
            Isambard Brunel Middle School

here is Portchester, Chichester Roads and Laburnum Grove
Emsworth Road, named after the nearby village
East Side
92   Mrs. M. Tebay, Grocer

West Side
57b   Solent Motors Ltd., Motor Engineers
77a   Dunne's Lock Up Garages

Epworth Road named after the home of the Wesley family because of the
church on the corner.

South Side
16   Gideon Lamb, Chiropodist

Farlington Road, named after nearby village
West Side
15   Frank Quinton, General Stores

here is Wymering Road
17   Albert Froud, Fried Fish Shop
39   Chapman's Laundry, Receiving Office

here are Portchester and Chichester Roads
Fearon Road, named after the Rev. Dr. Fearon Residential only.

Havant Road, named after the nearby town
West Side
9

"At number 9 lived Miss Voller a music teacher. My mother who was an excellent pianist of popular music, was self taught and wanted me to have the benefit of lessons. I really never wanted to go but off I went with my old music case and exercise book to practise scales. To me as a child the front room was dark and old fashioned. There was another girl who came, I believe her name was Susan. We would play a duet together. When Miss Voller was out of the room we would giggle and then be told off. I am afraid I was not the best of pupils, having to practise at home when I would hear my friends playing in the street was something I didn't enjoy. My mother eventually gave up on me. Needless to say I have lived to regret my time wasted with my piano teacher."
Margaret Webster

45   Mrs. S. A. Williams, Shopkeeper
57   Was earlier Taylor & Sons Dairies (1912) Ltd., Depot and later Norman Radford Commercial Vehicle sales.

here is Chichester Road
83   C. A. Meyer, Beer Retailer, Off Licence

Heathcote Road, named after Chancellor Heathcote? Residential only

Hewett Road
South Side
56   Portsea Island Mutual Co-operative Society, Grocers

North Side

77	Miss A. Pearce, Dressmaker
89	The Candy Stores, Grocers
	Portsmouth Civil Defence Centre, the site was later Battenburg Clinic and is now occupied by the child welfare offices.

Inhurst Road, earlier known as Occupation Road, Buryfield Lane and Priors Lane. Named after village near Winchester College. Occupation Roads were what would now be termed unadopted or private roads where the occupiers were responsible for the upkeep and usually were built by a landowner to provide personal access to his land. Residential only.

Kensington Road, named after the London district.
West Side
here is Laburnum Grove
57   Berkel Auto Scale Co Ltd.

here is Copythorn Road
59   A. Bryant, General Stores

here is Stubbington Avenue
81   Pettitt & Smith, Decorators

here are Kirby, Mayfield and Hewett Roads
East Side

here are Wallington and Epworth Roads
30   J. Wilkie, Grocer

here are Laburnum Grove, Copythorn Road and Stubbington Avenue
68   Mrs. E. G. Wallis, General Stores

here are Heathcote, Winton and Kirby Roads
Recreation Ground College Park, named after Winchester College who owned most of the land in the area as Stubbington Farm. The college gave the land to the town in 1915 to be used as a park. Like most parks and open areas there is a reason behind the use. Some parks are on very wet, marshy ground not suitable for building. Others like this have some communal facility, in this case a sewage pumping station and large electricity substation. The ground near the pumping station like that at Bransbury Park would be kept clear to allow for access to the pipework.

here are Mayfield, Domum and St Swithun's Roads
Kenyon Road, named after the Lord. Residential only

Kirby Road, named after Rev. Kirby.
South Side
28   H. Smith (Portsmouth) Ltd., Garage Proprietors, Office

here is Beresford Road
40   Rev. C. V. Corner, Methodist

here are Balfour, Fearon and Randolph Roads
92   H. Samuels, Teacher of Music
94   Mrs. C. Newboult, Teacher of Music
98   Rev. Pierce Deigan, Vicar of Ascension Church

here is Crofton Road
100   Rev. Bernard Thompson, Baptist

here are Lyndhurst, Kenyon, Chelmsford and Kensington Roads
172   Fred. Dashwood, Funeral Director, Dashwood & Sons

Laburnum Grove Was known as Brass Button Alley due to the Naval officers who lived there. Half way along the road at the junction with what is now Farlington Road was a turning circle where the road ended before being extended to Copnor Road. Local stories that this was the pond of Stubbington Farm are

incorrect as the pond was in what became the east side of Balfour Road, between Stubbington Avenue and Laburnum Grove.

South Side
here are Havant, Emsworth and Drayton Roads
58   North End School of Motoring

here are Beresford, Balfour, Beaulieu, Burlington and Farlington Roads
154   Victoria College, Miss V. Hibberd

here are Farlingon, Lyndhurst, Paddington, Belgravia and Kensington Roads
314a   A. Brading, Builder, Workshop
North Side
here are Emsworth and Drayton Roads
63   St. Margarets Day Nursery & Kindergarten School, Mrs. M. E. Vose
here are Beresford and Balfour Roads
171   Miss Lilian Finch, Teacher of Music. She was earlier in Chichester Road.
177   Mrs. G. N. Morris, Grocer

here are Lyndhurst and Kensington Roads

London Road
West Side
1-3   Inland Revenue (4th Income Tax District)
1-3A   Montague Burton Ltd., Tailors. The foundation stone bears the inscription "Raymond Montague Burton 1938". The shop opened on 30 September 1938. It was built by J. Moreton & Son of London. The shop has been divided up into smaller units and the upper floors were later used as a fitness centre and dancing school. The upper storeys plus a new storey have now been made into flats.
3   Herbert Osborne, Tobacconist. Survived until comparatively recently as an old fashioned tobacconist. The interior was removed and is stored in the City Museum.

"I found this shop fascinating all the different tobacco blends that you could smell inside the shop and also just walking past if the shop door was open. There were wooden cabinets with displays of pipes, lighters, cigarettes of all descriptions. We would go in there especially at Christmas for a special blend of Tobacco for my Uncle Den's pipe."

Margaret Webster

5	Willerby & Co. Ltd., Tailors
7-9	Boots The Chemists
11	W. H. Smith & Son Ltd., Booksellers
13	Smeeds Ltd., Wine Merchants
13A	J. H. Dewhurst Ltd., Butchers
15	At the rear the Myrtle Brewery was built in 1870 by William Stevens. It came under control of George King, the estate agent. In most cases property ended up with the agent due to failure to keep up the mortgage payments. It was rebuilt in 1878 as the Lion Brewery for King & Co. In the 1880s it was sold to members of the Young family of brewers. They sold it in 1902 and it was sold again in 1910 to Brickwoods. Later it was used as a factory by various companies before re-opening in 1982 as the Southsea Brewery. This closed in 1985. In 1996 the brewery tower was converted into flats and the outbuildings into houses.
17	Keyes, House Furnishers First listed in 1880 as a beer retailer. In the 1887 directory it is shown as the North Pole. Apart from that it was listed only as a beer retailer again until 1953. It then became a shop until 1977. A new pub was then opened in 1982 the Brewery Tap. Baptist Church In February 1894 the site in London Road was bought for £700, later in March additional land was bought for a further £130 by the church at Lake Road in order to provide for the growing population at North End. A Sunday school opened at the rear of the cottage in London Road and later became the hall for the church. On 29th January 1902 the foundation stones for the church were laid by Mr William Miller, Mr. Samuel Benney, Pastor G. Robert Hearn for the congregation, Mr. James Blake for Sunday school, Mr. & Mrs. John Palmer in memory of son John, Rev. W. H. Baker, Mrs. A. Porter in memory of Albert Porter. The church opened on the 24th of September 1902. The cost was £3,929 and the architect John Wills of Derby, the builder was Councillor J. W. Perkins. In 1904 the congregation separated from Lake Road Baptist Church. In 1923 the Sunday school was extended and the upper and outer hall built as First World War Memorials at a cost of £2,000 The church closed on 9th of December 2001 when the last service was held. The congregation amalgamated with Powerscourt Road Baptist, becoming North End Baptist. The building has since been converted into a public house, The Lanyard, a Smith and Jones house.
21	Charles of Bond Street, Ladies' Hairdressers

"Was a hairdresser in the sixties called Victors, my friend Jean introduced it to me, she had a short hairstyle called a 'Peek a Boo' hair either side of the ear."

Sylvia Webb

21   Mansfield & Sons Ltd., Boot Makers
25   Timothy Whites & Taylors Ltd., Chemists etc.
27   Campions (Bakers) Ltd.

here is Croft Road named after Pit Croft or Stamshaw Croft.

29	W. Pink & Sons Ltd., Grocers
31-33	George Victor, House Furnishers
35	G. Bateman., Opthalmic Optician Still there in 2005.
37	Lipton Ltd., Provision Merchants
39	Maypole Dairy Co. Ltd., Grocers
41-43	Marks & Spencer Ltd., Department Store
45	Was first listed as the Queen's Head at Kingston Cross. The pub was for sale as part of Henry Bransbury's estate in 1879. It was still listed as the Queen's Head in 1898. In 1906 there were plans to rebuild and in 1908 the pub was rebuilt at a cost of £1,300 Listed from 1910 to 1948 as the Polar Star from 1958 it is shown as shops. Above the shops you can still see the typical half-timbered facade of a Portsmouth Pub.
49	Sybil Stewart (Fashions) Ltd., Gowns
51	A. G. Cooper, Butcher
53	G. T. Cockayne, Restaurant
55	The British Bata Shoe Co. Ltd., Boot Makers
57	Smith & Sons (Portsmouth) Ltd., Bakers
59	Gaumont Cinema Licence granted in 1924 to Portsmouth Picture House (Portsmouth) Ltd. who opened it as the Regent Picture House, with 1908 seats. A Christie cinema organ was installed in 1929. Later it became part of the Gaumont chain. It closed and was demolished in 1974. Regent House and the parade of shops in front were also demolished. The site remained derelict until in 1992 the new shops and car park were built including the Presto Supermarket which became Safeways (then briefly Morrisons who then sold it to Somerfield).

"Earlier in my life, when I was courting the girl who was to become my first wife, I knew the manager of the Gaumont Cinema in London Road. We were both students at the Art College, and Mr Davies was a keen vegetarian, who joined the Portsmouth Vegetarian Group which I founded as our President. Whenever we wanted to visit the cinema, we only had to knock on his door to be given free admission, very helpful for struggling students. On one occasion, because there was a film on at the Odeon in Southsea which we wanted to see, Mr Davies made arrangements for us to get there free too! On a special occasion, when I organised an Animals' Fair at the Savoy Ballroom, Mr Davies used his connections to support us with gymnastics display by a team from the Women's League of Health and Beauty."

Mike Maybury

61-63   J. Sears & Co. (True Form Boot Co.) Ltd., Shoe Dealers
            Regent House. At one time home of the Young family who were related to the Whites by marriage. The Young family were brewers, estate agents and auctioneers.
            Refuge Assurance Co. Ltd.
            Neil Designs Ltd., Consultant Engineers
            Lectrotech (Gt. Britain) Ltd. Climatic Controls Ltd.

    "Leda Window Cleaners was run by the father of one of my boyfriend's ex-girlfriends, at Regent House. In the same building was Refuge Insurance where my next door neighbour, Maureen Guy, worked as a secretary; to our friend Pat's then fiancee's father, Mr Christie. (His son went on the run Christie Intruder Alarms) I would go there occasionally if I missed the door to door agent, as we were all sold Refuge Insurance if we were friends of Maureens."

Sylvia Webb

65   Saxone Shoe Co. Ltd.
67-69   Southern Gas Board Showrooms
71   Barnett-Hutton Ltd., Costumiers
73   Weston's (A. E. Hicks & Co. Ltd.), Bakers
75   National Assistance Board
77   Domestic Electric Rentals Ltd., Radio renting company
79   J. Baker & Co. Ltd., Outfitters. One of a chain of shops owned by one time M.P. John Baker for Portsmouth. They sold school, scout and guide uniforms.
St. Mark's Church.
            On the 30th of April 1868 the first meeting was held in the Clarence Gardens Music Hall. The foundation stone for the new church was laid on the 23rd of December 1872 by Bishop Wilberforce on a site given by Winchester College. The architect was Sir Arthur Blomfield. The church was consecrated on St. Mark's Day, 25th April 1874. The church was extended by the addition of a south aisle in 1889 and the tower was added in 1898. A new church was built on the opposite side of Derby Road on the site of the vicarage and consecrated in October 1970 and the old church demolished and a three storey block of shops and offices built on the site.

St. Mark's Church

here is Derby Road named after the Earl of Derby, Prime Minister

83-85	Hardy & Co., House Furnishers
87	W. Hartley & Co. Ltd., Naval & Civil Tailors & Outfitters
89	Sea Houses Ltd., Fishmongers & Poulterers
91	Direct Raincoat Co., Rainwear Later Stone-Dri, Rainwear, shoes, casual wear etc.
93	Milward & Sons Ltd., Shoe Retailers
95	Thatched House, William Lacey. First listed in 1867. It was a Miles Brewery house. Recently renamed Thatchers.
97	Lancia Fashions Ltd., Gowns Later Knitwear, lingerie, skirts, coats, dresses etc.
99	H. & S. Ford Ltd., Boot Repairers
101	Finlay & Co. Ltd., Tobacconists
103	Edgars, Men's Outfitters
105	Wendover & Co. Ltd., House Furnishers. A small branch of the Southsea company.
107	Percy Tuck, Newsagent, stationer, bookseller & tobacconist. Still a newsagents in 2005.
109	W. J. Stevens & Sons Ltd., Pork Butchers
111	Leddington (Portsmouth) Ltd., Butchers
113	Douglas Cooper Ltd., Chemist Still a chemist in 2005.
115-117	Watts, Fruiterers
119	The Chocolate King, Confectioners

here is Angerstein Road

An unusual name and the only Angerstein of note was John Julius Angerstein, who was born in St Petersburg in 1735. He emigrated to London in 1750 where he became one of the inspirations for Lloyds of London. A merchant, he lived in Pall Mall with a country residence, Woodlands, on the banks of the Thames. His collection of 38 paintings formed the start of the National Gallery in 1824. He was also a friend of Pitt the Younger. Why we should have a street named after him we have no idea although for a short time he owned Leigh Park House.

here is Gladys Avenue

In 1883 Mr. A. W. White in recognition of his services to the area the council allowed him to name a road, and he named it after his daughter who was born that year. Gladys White had a very eventful life which was written about some years ago in the Hampshire Magazine of January 1980.

121-123	Southdown Buildings. Although if you look up to the parapet you will see the initials STC, this was the Southsea Tourist Company who were later taken over by Southdown. These are built in the front garden of Mr. A. W. Whites house, the Poplars. The house can still be seen above the shops of London Road and Gladys Avenue.

Southdown Motor Services Ltd.

123	Linton's, Fancy Goods Dealers

Gladys Avenue

"Linton's, a handbag, luggage and accessories shop, was next door to the Southdown Offices. My then friend Meg Jackson took over the shop keeping the name and goodwill in 1977 and at Christmas I helped her to sell bags one Saturday. It was a little goldmine very busy at this time of year, she needed someone while she went to the back to hook down the bags which customers expressed interest in. There was a kitchen at the back. At the front was a glass showcase counter where all the purses, keyrings, wallets etc. were stored. It was run by her, and then her husband Colin finally closing in the eighties. They expanded the business to take over the old electricity office in Fratton Road but this was not so successful closing relatively quickly. Behind the bag shop was a home made wine shop, next door was a wallpaper shop. I still have wallpaper on the front room wall purchased from this shop, it is brown and silver, a tree design, which also looks like toffee paper."

Sylvia Webb.

125	G. W. Green Ltd., Bakers
125	Ministry of Transport, Driving Examiners
127	Worlds Stores Ltd., Grocers
129	H. C. Daley & Son, Jewellers & Silversmiths. Later was F. Hinds Ltd.

"I lived near the Daleys in Mark Close when they lived in Greenfarm Gardens in Hilsea. When the Daleys retired from Hinds, I was working with his son David and the whole family emigrated to South Africa. David was a happy person."

Sylvia Webb

here is the Promenade

131	Hipps Ltd., Tailors
133	D. Gold, Costumier
135	Brunswick Dyeing & Cleaning Co. Ltd. Another of Mr White's businesses.
137	Lipton Ltd., Provision Merchants
139	Verrecchia Ltd., Ice Cream Manufacturers & Milk Bar.
141	Parson's Trunk Stores (Hender & Sons Ltd)
143-147	Portsea Island Mutual Co-Operative Society Ltd., Grocers
149	Miss D. Middleton, Ladies' Outfitter
151	George Oliver (Footwear) Ltd.
153	C. J. Beaumont Ltd., Outfitters "Mens and Boys wear, footwear, overalls and camping equipment."
155	Hargreaves (Sports) Ltd., Athletic Outfitters, Toys & Games. They were agents for Meccano.
157-159	Southern Electricity Board, Showrooms
161	Field (Cleaners) Ltd., Dyers & Cleaners

163	Fountain, John Garnett First listed in 1805 as The Fountain Inn, London Road. It was rebuilt in 1898 or 1900 depending which book you believe to designs of local architect A. E. Cogswell. It was a originally a Spicer's brewery house.
165	R. S. Cheshire Ltd., Opticians

"My mother decided on Cheshire's Opticians and I liked it because of the Lucky Black Cat in the window. The opticians were good and polite, opening the door as you left."

Here is Connaught Road named after the Duke of Connaught

167-169	George Hodges, Motor Cycle Agent
171	Samuel Sanders, Fried Fish Shop Still a Fish and Chip shop in 2005.
173	Bush & Tidy, Auctioneers, Estate Agents & Valuers
175	George Hodges, Cycle Agent
177	R. G. Wills, Confectioner
179	William O'Brien, Ladies' Hairdresser
181	George Bentley Ltd., Electrical Engineers
183	Longlife Battery Depot
185	North End Photographic Store, Photographic dealers. Was a photographic shop for many years under various names.

"My dad bought his cameras, cine projector and screen there. The assistants were always helpful and knew what to advise you. I remember Dad's first Cine was very heavy but it was always taken on every holiday."

Margaret Webster

187	Leonard Evans, (Ophthalmic Opticians) Ltd.
189	Campbells, House Furnishers

here is Munster Road

191	Smith & Smith, Estate Agents. Now Todd & Hartridge Estate Agents. Also Hildreths School of Motoring
197	Rex Parish and Gerald Murray, Ophthalmic Opticians
199-201	James Bryant & Son (Portsmouth) Ltd., Motor Engineers. No longer a filling station and garage but used by Kwik Fit.
203	Auto Services, Motor Car Agents

"North End Motors on the corner of London Road and London Avenue was run by Boothby Bros., Claude and Brian Boothby. My friend, Pamela, married Claude, and Claude was also best man at my wedding to David Webb"

Sylvia Webb

here is London Avenue

205	William McEldowney, Dental Surgeon
217	Russell Checks, Credit Check Traders
229	Hollings, Hughlings & Son, Solicitors & Commissioners for Oaths

here is North End Avenue

233	Swift Radio & Television Service, Radio Engineers
235	Walter Legg & Son, Boot Repairers
237	Edwin Tanner, Umbrella Maker
241	Chapman's Laundry Receiving Office
243	D. Cleverley, Ironmonger
247	Mrs. J. Harrison, Dolls Hospital. The Dolls Hospital later moved to New Road on the corner with Balliol Road. In 1967 Edmund and Vera Rosenkranz opened "Paddy's Parlour". The cooking was supervised by Vera, who was from Charleville, County Cork. She trained at the Victoria Hotel, Cork and afterwards at Wicklow, Dublin.

"Paddy's Parlour Restaurant. In 1967 when it was my boyfriend's birthday I booked a table at Paddy's Parlour, and it was mid-week, we went along earlyish because we had to get up in the morning and we were the only two there, the food and service was excellent though. I read an advertisement 19th May 1981 in the News saying more about Paddy who was in fact a Pole. Paddy played the violin at the restaurant, the violin had first been played by his grandfather Franz under the baton of Johann Strauss in Vienna. Edmund trained as a chef at Highbury. Meals were £4 a la carte etc."

Sylvia Webb

here is Wadham Road, named after the Oxford University college.

249	Lloyds Bank Ltd
251	A. F. C. Coppin, Physician & Surgeon. Now Pratt's Harbour Veterinary Services.
259 & 267	Central Distributors (Southern) Ltd, Refrigerator dealers
271	Co-operative Insurance Society Ltd.

here is Oriel Road, named after the Oxford University college.

275	London Road Stores, C. Chubb, Grocers
277	Hy. Harris & Dennis Jackman, Physician & Surgeons
285	E. G. Cotterall Ltd., Ladies' hairdressers
287	A. S. Terribile, Dispensing Optician

here is Shadwell Road, possibly named after a Provost of Oriel College.

291-293	The Excel, Fried Fish Caterers. Still a fish and chip shop in 2005.

297-299	Smith & Vosper Ltd., Grocers
301	Elton-Walters, Grocers
303	Frederick Milmer, Newsagent
305	Ophir Garage, Motor Engineers & Garage. Still a petrol station in 2005.

here is Ophir Road, named after the Oxford University College

311	Miss J. Barnard, Confectioner
313	Rechabite Buildings Royal Naval District Independent Order of Rechabites British Israel Hall Built in 1931. Listed as the British Israel Hall until 1962, then from 1964 to 1983 as the Church of Latter Day Saints. They transferred to Kingston Crescent and houses were built on the site after demolition in 1990.
315	Mrs. May Abbott, Greengrocer
315	Hilsea Mission Listed from 1948 to 1960 as Hilsea Mission
321	Denniss & Partners, Dental Surgeons
325	Frederick Manning, Fishmonger
329	Alfred Voller (S. Hutchings), Butcher
335	Tunbridge Wells Equitable Friendly Society
337A	Stanley Primmett, Furniture Remover
337	Provident Clothing & Supply Co. Ltd., Credit Drapers

here is Magdalen Road, named after the Oxford University college.

371	The Green Posts, James Kille. In 1748 the corporation leased it to

London Road, North End

the brewery for a 1,000 years at 13s 4d a year. Listed as The Green Post in 1748. It has also been the Green Post Inn and the Green Posts. It was a Pike Spicer Brewery house. Named after the boundary of Portsmouth prior to 1832. The Green Post was replaced by the stone obelisk standing in the grounds of the car sales pitch opposite. The area to the north was prior to the boundary change part of Wymering.

here is Meredith Road, named after the local author, George Meredith.

373-383	G. A. Day Ltd., Builders' Merchants. Started as a haulier and expanded into building materials, including brick making at Burrfields, where the business is now located, recently changing to Days Buildbase following the sale of the business.
385	Daytona Wholesale Electrical Ltd.
	Kipling Buildings

here is Kipling Road, named after author Rudyard Kipling who was schooled in Portsmouth

415	Valer, Ladies' Hairdressers
	Doyle Court

here is Doyle Avenue, named after Dr. Conan Doyle author of the Sherlock Holmes stories

Near here was earlier the Kings Head Brewery

509	Rev. Arthur Allcock, Chaplain of Royal Garrison Church
511	Large eighteenth century two storey house built of red and grey bricks, with architrave framed windows surmounted by flat gauged arches and panelled door in porch with doric columns and pediment. It was entirely rebuilt in 1983.

"In the late seventies, early eighties I worked at Avenue House, Hilsea, as a volunteer tutor teaching English as a second language. My first pupils were both from North Vietnam, two young women with young babies and husbands. At first I was nervous as neither women could speak any English. They were so grateful to be in England that it was a joy to teach them. They with other Vietnamese of all ages made Avenue House their home whilst waiting for permanent homes in various parts of the country. I remember sitting in the kitchen with everyone preparing food. It was my first experience of Vietnamese food which I liked. Talking of food whilst in a classroom with pupils talking about farm animals. It was the first time I realised that in certain parts of the world, dog was also on the menu. Later my next two pupils were from South Vietnam, both men had left their wives and children behind. These students were not happy to be in England and had wanted an American Skipper to have rescued them. By and large although they could speak some English they did not really want to work at English or general housework. All they though about was America, I often wondered how they faired."

Margaret Webster

513   J. F. Ginn, Chiropodist

here are Southwood, Beechwood, Elmwood & Oakwood Roads.
Named since they are built on the site of Oak Farm. Farmers are listed as from 1859 to 1867 Elizabeth Ellis, in 1886 William Harry Stephens, then from 1910 to 1913 Harry Cheesman. In 1918 Charles Dye had a brickfield here. Some of the old farm buildings remained for many years and were visible from Hartley Road. Portsmouth Technical High School.

"Originally started at the Municipal College behind the Guildhall in Park Road in 1913 as The Junior Technical School. Later changing its name to The Technical School. It was located for a time in the Portsea Parish Institute opposite St Mary's Church in Fratton Road and later at rooms behind the Congregational Church on the corner of Queens Road and Kingston Road. An eventual home for the school was found at the Art College at Hilsea on the London Road (opposite the Coach and Horses Public House), sharing the buildings on the site. During the Second World War the pupils of the school were evacuated to the Salisbury area. In 1958 the school was amalgamated with The Portsmouth Building School to form The Technical High School. The Building School was formed during the Second World War from pupils that had stayed in the city. It was realised that after the war there would be a great need for skilled workers to rebuild the nation and there would be a dire shortage of skilled artisans particularly in the building and allied trades. Therefore the need for a school for pupils of a particular aptitude towards such trades. In a short while after the amalgamation the Art College moved to another location in the city and the school took over the whole site. In the years previous to the amalgamation new buildings were added to the site, particularly the Central Science Block, Assembly Hall and the Gymnasiums. Later the workshops at the rear of the site were constructed replacing wooden huts originally on the site. The school colours for The Technical School was black and white, the tie being alternate colours. One form of the tie being horizontal stripes the other the more conventional diagonal stripes. The colours for the Building School were red and white. The colours for The Technical High School combined all three colours of black, red and white. The tie was mainly black with thin red diagonal stripes with two very thin white stripes within the red stripes. The badge of The Technical School was a medieval ship with sails furled with the star and crescent moon either side of the mast. This device was taken from the original seal of the town of Portsmouth and modified for the badge of the school. The Building School badge was the Phoenix rising from the ashes, depicting the rebuilding of the city after the war. The Technical High school combined both badges half of each occupying each half of a shield with the city's star and crescent above, with an open book on one side and a set square and compass on the other. Whilst the earlier schools had a smaller replica of the coat badge as a cap badge, it was decided that for the Technical High School, the cap being black with red and white stripes around the cap was distinctive on its own and therefore did not require a cap badge. Other sites that were used prior and during amalgamation in the late 1950's were at Greetham Street near the Guildhall Square and the High Street in Cosham. These were workshops for painting and decorating and bricklaying and plastering and were closed when the new workshops were opened on the Hilsea site. In the 1980's during a reorganisation of the city's education, the name was changed to The City of Portsmouth Boys School. The badge of The Technical High School, being retained for the new school."

Peter Galvin

Southern College of Art (Hilsea Annexe)
Express Electrical Services, Automobile electrical engineers

here is Northwood Road, part of the Oak Farm estate.

	United Service Garages (Portsmouth) Ltd. Hilsea Market
9	William Harvell, Cycle Dealer "He was an ex-Olympic Cyclist"
10	Joseph Franklin, Butcher
11	Leach & Bartlett Ltd., Provision Merchants
12	William Causby, Newsagent & Post Office
13	William Ruffell, Fruiterer
14	C. Payne, Fishmongers
14	Portsbridge Cafe, Restaurant

here are Hilsea Crescent and Northern Parade

Portsmouth Grammar School Playing Fields

Southdown Motor Services Ltd., Depot Bastion Service Station, E.M.A Ltd.

Hilsea Swimming Pool and Hilsea Recreation Grounds. In September 1934 the lowest tender for construction of a new swimming baths of £26,285 was accepted. On 25 July 1935 they were opened by the Lord Mayor. The complex consisted of a 220ft open air pool which cost £40,000 with 10m diving tower. Cafe, with dance floor, childrens splash pool, skating rink and boating lake.

"My first memories of Hilsea Lido are being a child and walking with my Mum and dog, Judy, to Alexandra Park. Along the shore seeing boys doing unspeakable things to crabs. The freshwater stream was always fascinating to us children, Dad would explain all about the many creatures to be found there.

In those days Hilsea Lido was a special place to go, a boating lake, crazy golf, skating, swimming pool, paddling pool, beautiful terraced rose gardens and cafe,. Many happy hours were spent there, at weekends and holidays too always seemed to be very crowded. I'm sure that many romances were started and finished there. It seems that for many years Hilsea Lido has been a lost opportunity."

Margaret Webster

"My first recollections of Hilsea Lido were a as boy when my friends and I would pass over Portsbridge on our rambling adventures into the open country side that surrounded Portsmouth. It was then open space with Hilsea Council Estate being built in Northern Parade and the Lido swimming pool just being completed. To our young eyes it was a marvellous site - a glimpse into a new world we had only seen at the cinema. Not that we could afford to swim there - ours was a far bigger pool, the sea, where we could enjoy ourselves without paying when ever we were able to, meeting our friends from where we lived in Landport. The rest of this beautiful area was being developed being gardens, tennis courts, a boating lake in the rampart moat, plus a restaurant where you could buy cups of tea, ice cream and other refreshments through a shop window built into the wall of the building and enjoy being seated in an open area where chairs and tables were provided. This building also contained a large dining hall with a stage, dance floor and modern kitchens in all, a very welcome addition to the social and recreational assets of the City run directly

Miniature Railway at Hilsea Lido

28

Hilsea Lido

by the then Parks Department. Over the years, due to persistent neglect by Portsmouth City Council it has become run down an d a shadow of its former beautiful self. An amenity likely to become a commercial asset of a contracting company to be developed and lost forever as a social facility in the northern part of the City and what we knew as a beautiful recreational municipal asset that we had enjoyed become an historical memory. I recall going as a family and hiring a boat on the moat enjoying a lovely Sunday afternoon with much laughter and a sense of adventure for both adults and children. At this time you would see newly married couples having their wedding group photographs taken whilst they posed on the bridge over the moat with the trees etc. making a marvellous background. When I retired in 1984 we held my retirement party in the Blue Lagoon - the restaurant on the Lido site, tickets were sold and the hall was filled to its capacity. The three course meal was excellent but when some my friends from Portsmouth Players started to present the cabaret a leg fell off the half sized grand piano and the staff had to effect an emergency repair with a lump of wood and rope! An event which occasioned much laughter and good humour from the audience. It was a marvellous evening, the venue was perfect, a memory to be always cherished by all who were there."

Frank Deacon

"When I was younger I lived at the Lido in the summer. Going first to the paddling pool. I had two secondhand bathing costumes, the first one a dark green woollen one which I ruined going down the slide into the water. For the big pool a floral patterned one. We first went to the Lido with my parents who liked to walk from Cosham around the shore to Alexandra Park after spending time at the Lido and bus back or vice versa. I learned to swim at the Guildhall baths with the school and at Hilsea Lido with my friends. I was scared of getting out of my depth and made the mistake of standing chatting to boys we knew at the big slide which was by the deep end, 10 foot mark which was the deepest part of the pool and I was pushed in. One time going to the Lido with friends we all had the same locker in the changing rooms and we left it so we could go back for things and everything was stolen from the locker. I got no sympathy from my mother who gave me nought out of ten for common sense. At the Lido I stayed in the shallow end at first until I learned to swim. It always got so crowded with people diving in from everywhere or jumping in. I especially liked the fountain end although it had been seized up for many years."

East Side

2	Blue Anchor Hotel, Harry Marsh. Listed in 1715 as the Blue Anchor, Kingston. From 1830 it is listed at Kingston Cross. It was rebuilt in 1884 to the designs of local architect A. E. Cogswell and became 2 London Road. In 1940 it was one of the first buildings to be bombed. After the war it was reduced to a single storey building.
4-6	Nelsons, House Furnishers. Was earlier Taylor & Sons Dairies (1912) Ltd., Restaurant & Ice Cream Manufacturers. Listed in 1898 as Taylor & Sons, and Kingston Cross Dairies. In 1912 the company became limited. In 1939 they amalgamated with other local dairies to form Portsmouth Dairies.
8	National Provincial Bank Ltd. Biscoe-Smith & Blagg, Solicitors & Commissioners for Oaths
10	City of Portsmouth Public Libraries (North End Branch). This was upstairs and was a traditional 'old fashioned' library. It was replaced by the new library in Gladys Avenue. City Police Station Built in 1896 it was replaced by the new station in nearby Kingston Crescent which opened in 1963, combining with Fratton Station.
12	Asher Henry Ltd., Rainwear
14	Dorothy Perkins Ltd., Drapers

"Always had a very attractive window display. If you wanted special underwear this was the shop to go to. They sold from glass topped counters that had drawers underneath."

Margaret Webster

16	Corbin's Shoe Retailers

here is Chichester Road, named after the Sussex City.

18	Midland Bank Ltd. Still a bank in 2005.
	Southern Counties Car Finance Corporation Ltd
20	Freeman, Hardy & Willis Ltd., Boot Makers
22-24	Bulpitt's Ltd., Drapers, Soft Furnishings and Ladies' Outfitter. They were bombed out of Kings Road and moved to 12 London Road, and then further north in London Road into the building formerly occupied by Jacobs, Furnishers, and later Woolworth.

"In the sixties they had a tropical fish tank in the fitment where the building turned towards Chichester Road that kept the children occupied while their mothers were browsing in the store. My mother always liked looking through the remnants to see if there were any pieces large enough to make skirts and aprons from. Like many other large stores they also had a central cashier and the money would be put into a canister and 'fired' on overhead wires from the sales counter to the cashier and back."

Stephen Pomeroy

26	Mason & Bennett Ltd., Outfitters
28-32	Will Brown (Portsmouth) Ltd., Soft Furnishings, floor coverings, drapers, milliners & ladies' outfitters. 'For value, service and variety.'
34	Walter J. Rugg & Co. Ltd., Tobacconist
34A	Maison Marcel's (Southsea) Ltd., Ladies' Hairdressers
36	Mrs. Dorothy Cooper, Milliner
38	Lloyds Bank Ltd. Still there in 2005. Here at the turn of the century was the blacksmith for the North End area.
40	John Temple Ltd., Tailors
42	Winchester Catering Co. Ltd, Caterers
44	Crown Wallpapers (Wallpaper Stores Ltd.)
46	Mac Fisheries Ltd., Fishmongers
48	Currys Ltd., Cycles, Radio and Television
50	Henry Playfair Ltd., Boot & Shoe Stores
52	Oswald Bailey (Southern) Ltd., Army & Navy Stores, naval, military & civilian outfitters, travel goods and camping equipment
54-58	Belmonts (Portsmouth) Ltd., Costumier, Milliner and Gown Specialist. Was part of James Messenger's family, they also had a cottage at the rear occupied by the coachman, as well as the jewellers shop on the corner of Laburnum Grove. The shop closed in October 1970. The shop was demolished in the 1980s and McDonalds now occupies the site.

"I looked in Portsmouth, London and Southampton for my wedding dress and at last saw something at Belmont in North End, it was in white dralon, a coat dress with sparkly diamante, looking buttons. Quite expensive but the only one I had seen that I liked."

Sylvia Webb

"Belmonts was a very special shop to my mother and myself. We loved looking in the window. It was a shop with class, when you entered an assistant greeted you and you were taken to your own cubicle. Then you would tell the assistant what you were looking for and clothes would be brought to you. If I remember correctly the assistant had a very good eye for what suited you or did not. I bought my wedding dress there which was pure silk, classic style. After all these years the design of the dress would not look out of place today. My mother bought her wedding outfit there. You were made to feel very special. Looking back to all the quality and specialised shops that there were in North End it seems impossible to believe."

Margaret Webster

60	Flowercrafts, Florists
62	J. Davidson, Gowns
64	Bellman's Wools, Wool stores
66	Howard's (Portsmouth) Ltd., Radio Engineers
68	Westminster Bank Ltd.
70	Boyds of Bond Street, Piano dealers. Was earlier Godfrey & Co. Ltd., Piano, Radio & Music Dealers. Established in 1859. 'Godfrey's brightened your dark evenings.'
72-74	Portsmouth Trustee Savings Bank. Now the Sir John Baker, public house.
76	J. & M. Stone, Radio Dealers
78	Barclays Bank Ltd. Now on the corner at number 82, 2005.
80	Smith & Vosper Ltd., Pastrycooks
82	James Messenger, Goldsmith, Jeweller & Watchmaker

here is Laburnum Grove

84	Weston Hart Ltd., Wireless Engineer & Gramophone Dealer.

"They sold records from pop to classical, radios, televisions etc. You could listen to the records in one of several booths before making up your mind to buy it. Over the years the shop got larger as it took in more of the rooms at the rear"

Stephen Pomeroy

86-88	Vacant in 1960, in previous years it had been Keast's Baby Carriages, then by 1962 it was Victor Value Co Ltd., grocers who were later taken over by Tesco's. The shop is currently Iceland.

Was earlier Thomas Humphries the local photographer. Looking above the shops here you can see the windows of the houses that were here earlier. The pavement is on what were the front gardens before the road was widened.

90   Silver Arrow Cleaners Ltd.

92   Fleming, Reid & Co. Ltd., Scotch Wool Stores

94   Odeon Theatres Ltd, Patrick Reed, Manager. Opened 14th December 1936, seating 1824. In recent years has been divided up into a number of smaller screens, at first three, then four.

"My friend Mary Roberts worked at the Odeon as an usherette, she worked in the ticket office and sold ice cream etc. We used to get two complimentary tickets a week which was nice as long as it lasted, Mary changed jobs quite a lot."

Sylvia Webb

96   Paige Gowns Ltd., Ladies Wear. Here were large houses set well back from the road. The site was developed and became the new premises for Woolworths.

98   F. W. Woolworth & Co. Ltd

"I worked here in the sixties. At that time the store was much bigger with counters and assistants standing behind them, even a delicatessen. It certainly seemed to be a much busier store than it is today, Saturdays and especially Christmas it was packed. I worked on the haberdashery which I found boring but towards spring I was transferred to bulbs and packets of seeds. It was always very hectic. Woolworths had a good reputation for their quality. Certain customers who were well known would come into the shop the last five minutes before closing and linger. The most annoying customer was the person usually female who could see you were serving a customer but constantly called out 'Miss' and would then tap, tap on the glass counter."

Margaret Webster

"Woolworths had large wooden four sided counters for each department. The staff entered in gaps in the corners. The tops were divided up into sections with plate glass dividers joined with metal clips. A clip at the rear of each section had the price tag. There were counters for electrical, toys, gardening, stationary, sweets, records, housewares, tools, grocery, delicatessen, ladies wear, childrens wear etc. The shop was a lot larger than it is now going further back and deliveries were made to the rear entrance."

Stephen Pomeroy

98a   Rentaset Ltd., Radio Renting

100	Miss Violet May, Blouse Specialist
102	Stylo Boot Co. Ltd., Boot Makers

"This was where I bought my first pair of very pointed black leather high heels. So I forced my feet into a size smaller. I lived to regret this as I soon found myself with corns on both little toes. As my mother was against my buying the shoes she was never told of the agony I was in. I can still feel the pain now!"

Margaret Webster

104	Smeeds Ltd., Wholesale & Retail Wine, Spirit & Beer Merchants. Still an off licence in 2005.
106	Andre, (of North End), Ladies' Hairdressers. "They also sold perfume at Christmas."
108	Beverley Cafe, Later this was Cantoys Newsagents and Confectioners
110	Stella (M. Marodeen), Costumier
114	Beagley, Wool Shop
116	Carlisles', Florists
118	Clarence Gardens, Arthur Spencer. Listed in 1716 as The Land Of Promise and in 1773 a house called Land Of Promise and Pleasure Gardens are mentioned in deeds of the area. It was still known as the Land of Promise in 1844. By 1847 it had become the Clarence

Stubbington Avenue, North End

Gardens, North End and then in 1859 as the Clarence Gardens, Clarence Terrace. In 1860 Blondin walked across a rope in the tea gardens. It has changed name several times being the Clarence Tavern and Clarence Gardens over the years. In 1937 it was partly rebuilt to designs of local architect A. E. Cogswell. Renamed The Mischief in 2005 after refurbishment. As the Land of Promise it had gardens which stretched back to Emsworth Road and included a boating lake, fountains, statues etc.

"The landlady was always very well dressed - like a film star"
Sylvia Webb, Peter James

120   A. W. White & Co Ltd., House Furnishers, Furniture Removers & Storers. White & Co Ltd., Furniture Removers & Storers and Shipping Agents. Mr White was a railway agent and carrier and a prominent local businessman, who had interests in various areas. He was the man behind both Provincial Tramways at Fareham & Gosport, Portsmouth Trams (before they were taken over by the Corporation), he is also the White of many local firms :- Young & White, Bailey & White etc. (But not White & Newton)

here is Stubbington Avenue
This was originally the lane which led to Stubbington Farm; the farmhouse of which stood approximately where the Ascension Church is now.

122-124   Portsea Island Mutual Co-operative Society Ltd. On this corner was earlier a large house, one of the last occupants was Sir John Baker the M.P. for Portsmouth who had a chain of outfitting shops. The house was demolished in the 1920s and Melanies department store built. The Co-op later took over the shop. The Co-op moved out of the shop and it stood derelict for many years before burning out one morning in 1984.

"One December morning I met my boyfriend and we went for a coffee at Melanies and he proposed to me. We then went to the travel agents to book our holiday, now honeymoon. Later at Southsea, the other two who made up the foursome when we first went out together, Peter and Susan got married. We usually parked the car or cars, depending how many were going out together, in Stubbington Avenue, to go to the Clarence Arms or the Odeon Cinema. I remember having to look at the colour of the houses just inside Stubbington Avenue to get an idea for decoration and we were also into flock wallpaper"
Sylvia Webb

126	Halford Cycle Co. Ltd.
128	Cyril Purches, Men's Tailors, Outfitters & Hosiers
130	W. Fielder & Sons, Cutlers

"As well as cutlery they sold penknives, sheaf knives, magnifiers, glass and silverware."

132	H. Wain & Sons Ltd., Greengrocers
134A	Caesars Club. Later Oasis and Gatsby's.

"When it was the Oasis Club my brother used to play folk music with guitar and mouth organ on a frame which he made while doing overtime at Dragonaire at Farlington. Jon Isherwood and Pat Nelson were regular folk artists too. The first car that my brother owned, a Morris 1000, was bought from Pat Nelson. I have been to the Oasis to listen to folk music in the 1960s and to Gatsby's in the 1980s. For many years there were two post boxes outside to deal with estate agents post."

Sylvia Webb

136	Young & White, Auctioneers, Valuers, Surveyors & Estate Agents
138	McIlroys Ltd., Furnishing & Floor Coverings. They came here after being bombed out of premises in Commercial Road. After they opened a shop in the Tricorn they went bankrupt and the premises were used by Handyman and MFI before remaining closed for many years. The premises have recently re-opened as Montagues with small businesses renting space in the building and soon after changed to Willows. Flats have been made in the upper floors. Reputedly there is a spring under the building which still has to be pumped out.

"I have a biscuit barrel which was purchased there. We always used to look around because we once had neighbours called McIlroys who we liked."

Sylvia Webb.

here is Montague Road

144	Waterfield & Stanford, House, Land & Estate Agents
146	F. A. Harvey Ltd., Hardware Dealers
148	Harrow Stores (Watford) Ltd, Credit Drapers
152	L. Zeffertt & Sons Ltd., Tailors & Naval Outfitters
154	William McCammon, House Furnishers
156	Thompson's (Portsmouth) Ltd., Decorators' Merchants

"Thompsons was a paint and wallpaper showroom. Giving people ideas how to decorate their homes. Eventually taken over by his son Norman, then by Walpamur Ltd., then Crown Paints and eventually Reed International. Norman's son Tony was the Police Officer in charge when H.M & H.R.H opened Fratton Community Centre. Thompsons had two other shops where the real work was done. They were in Somers Road North. One for paint halfway along the road and the paper shop on the corner near the railway bridge. After a few years and the addition of two other shops the business moved to Fisher's Grove, Farlington."

Anton Cox

158	House of Wools
158	A. E. Manchip & Co. Ltd., Removal Contractors

"They had a model furniture van in the window."

160	Portsea Island Mutual Co-Operative Society Ltd., Opticians
162-164	South Coast Furnishing Co. Ltd.

here is Kirby Road, named after Rev Kirby

168	Larcome & Winter, Solicitors & Commissioners for Oaths, incorporating Kent & Co. John Winter, Albert Larcome, Julian Linington and Neville Winter.
170	F. G. Motors (Eric Barron), Motor Dealers

here is Thurbern Road

176	Yarborough Maternity & Medical Nursing Home, Miss K. Coleman, matron. This was demolished and the new headquarters for Portsmouth Building Society built on the site.
178	First Church of Christ Scientist. The original church was in Old Portsmouth in an old Methodist Church that was later bombed.

The new church here was built in 1956 although meetings on the site commenced in 1946 according to the trade directories.

here is Mayfield Road

198	North End Launderette Ritestar Ltd., The 'Eternor' Pen, Ball Pen Makers
200	Mrs. Lilian Dollery, Ladies' Hairdresser
204	A. Black & Mrs. Black, Veterinary Surgeons
208	L. E. Jones, Insurance Broker
214	Norman Innes, Solicitor & Commissioner for Oaths
	June Forsyth, Dental Surgeon

here is Inhurst Road first listed in 1910 as Occupation Road, then from 1912 to 1913 as Buryfield Road. It was later split in two the part from London Road to Randolph Road becoming Inhurst Road, the part from Randolph Road, Priors Lane.

218	G. & G. Curtis Ltd., Grocers
220	Falcon School of Motoring
222	C. Vernon Proctor, Printer & Stationer
224	Herbert Pain, Butcher
226	Jaffas, Greengrocers
228	Renwick, Wilton & Dobson Ltd., Travel Agents
230-232	G. Hardacre Ltd., Printers, Commercial Stationers, Typewriters and Office Equipment
234	John Fisher (Rider Agent) Ltd., Motor Car Agents and Dealers
236	Television Security Ltd., Television Dealers
	Vernon Court flats with shops under
238	R. W. H. Allway, Confectioner
240-244	John Fisher Ltd., Motor Cycle Agents

here is Hewett Road

292	Wesleyan & General Assurance Society Hemsley & Strugnell, Accountants
294	Norman Banks Ltd., Dispensing Chemist
310	Liss, Ladies' Hairdresser

here is St Chad's Avenue Shackleton House, named after the explorer.

326	George Peters & Co. Ltd., Wine Merchants
328	Andre, (of North End) Ltd., Ladies' Hairdressing
330	National Provincial Bank Ltd

"I started my first job working as the junior clerk in this branch. Mr Wagstaff was the manager and me joining put the staff up to five. The only machine we used was a mechanical adding machine. All ledgers were handwritten and statements were typed from them the next day. All cheques for other branches and banks were sent to London daily (except those received on Saturday which were sent with Mondays). One of my jobs was to take all postal orders to the Post Office near Torrington Road who gave me cash for them. Suits were worn Monday to Friday but it was expected that you would wear a sports jacket on Saturdays. You had about one Saturday in four off. The branch was altered while I was there giving me one good payday as I was there with the builders on a Sunday afternoon. My salary in 1961 was £224 a year."

Alan Eamey

here is Battenburg Avenue
332	Pankhurst (Weymouth) Ltd., Motor Cycle Specialists
338	Miss Joan Stoneham, Teacher of Dancing, Rathgar Hall
340	G. Stent, Road Traffic Consultant
344	Edward Morrison, Physician & Surgeon
350	Vita Dry Cleaners Ltd.
352	Rapid Repair Shoe Co.
356	Loyal Providential & Humane Lodge of Oddfellows Holloways Enquiry Office
362	William Morris, Tailor
364	B. M. Berg, Watchmaker
370	Jeffery Davies, Dental Surgeon
374	Arthur Steyn , Physician & Surgeon
382	Shawcross Service Station. Shawcross was an old name for this area of the island. Now a car sales pitch. The boundary stone of the town still stands in the grounds.

here is Torrington Road, named after the village.
402	Norman Humphrey, Chemist
404	W. Gould Ltd., Tobacconist & Post Office
406	Marie, Wool Store, Baby Linen, Ladies' Wear & Haberdashery
408	Debonair (S. Rogers) Hairdressers
410	Arthur Cooper, Wine & Spirit Merchants
412	John Tolhurst, Fishmonger
414	W. J. Stevens & Son Ltd., Butchers
416	Empire Fruits, Greengrocers
418	I. & L. Hopcraft, Grocers
420	Smith & Sons (Portsmouth) Ltd., Bakers
422	E. Mussell, Confectioner
424	Mayfare Cleaners

here is Merrivale Road
428	Glen-Roy Stores (John McNeill), High Class Grocers

434	Miss C. R. Buckle, Cafe,
440	Amberley Library (W. H. Mitchell), Newsagents
442	H. G. Luker, Baker
450	Frederick Andrews & Son, Hardware Stores. Later Amberley Stores. Still a hardware shop in 2005.
456	Portsea Island Mutual Co-operative Society, Grocers

here is Amberley Road, named after the village
Hilsea Barracks.

Dates back to 1587 when the area was used as a training ground for volunteers to defend the port against the Spanish Armada. Later in 1756 temporary buildings were erected for use by the Royal Marine Light Infantry. The site became a transit camp in 1783 and in 1794 was enlarged. In 1815 the buildings were taken down and much of the land sold. Originally the barracks extended much further south to almost Battenburg Avenue. In 1854 permanent buildings were erected for Royal Field Artillery and in 1921 the Royal Army Ordnance Corps moved here. During the war from 1942 to 1945 the barracks were used by the American Forces. The barracks closed and were sold for housing following the final parade by the R.A.O.C on the 20th October 1960. Gatcombe Park Housing Estate now occupies the site. In the barracks were two churches, one Church of England, one Roman Catholic both named St Barbaras, the Patron Saint of Gunners. At the north end of the area stood an elm tree, now marked by a stone block, under which John Wesley preached when he came to Portsmouth.

"Just to the north of the main entrance to Hilsea Barracks was a lane that ran from London Road through to Copnor Road and was called Record Road. This was a private road belonging to the MOD and was closed on high days and holidays as is the tradition for government owned land. About halfway along this lane met another lane which went to Old London Road. At this junction was an Army Hut which was the meeting place for the local Army Cadet Force, Hilsea Platoon B Company 17) Battalion The Royal Hampshire Cadet Force. The cadets used to meet for many years in this hut. When the RAOC (Royal Army Ordnance Corps) was in situ at Hilsea Barracks the ACF adopted the shoulder flashes and cap badges of the RAOC. The RAOC moved out of Hilsea in about 1960 and the troop reverted back to the Royal Hampshire flashes and cap badges. The cadets met on a weekly basis with the occasional weekend camps away either in the New Forest or on Salisbury Plain. The annual camp was taken the first week in August with all the Cadets from Hampshire and the IOW going away for the week to an army camp, somewhere like on Salisbury Plain or to Cornwall. The Hilsea Platoon consisted of two adult officials, lieutenants, ex warrant officers, an adult Sergeant Major, ex army other rank, a Cadet Sergeant, several Corporal and the rest privates."

Peter Galvin

here is Old London Road

Waring (Contractors) Ltd., Building & Civil Contractors

Highbury Cars (Portsmouth) Ltd., Motor Car Agents

Reading & Co. Ltd., Coach Builders

J. Sparshatt & Sons (Portsmouth) Ltd., Motor Vehicle Agents

Coach & Horses, Albert Grubb. This is at least the third public house in the area. The first one was built as a barracks pub on the southern end of the road in Old London Road but was burnt down in 1872. The new building was erected at the north and survived until 1908. In 1907 the government were in the process of selling all the government owned pubs and also reducing the number of pubs. The licence for the building was revoked while the brewery were in the process of paying £10,000 for the premises. As this represented the value of the licenced business the whole affair went to Parliament and after much publicity in the press the government pubs that had been sold were allowed to keep their licences. To commemorate the event the sign was painted on the side of the pub showing the Chancellor of the Exchequer as a Highwayman holding up the coach containing the owner of the brewery, hence the Coach & Horses. When the pub was rebuilt in 1931 the sign was reproduced in ceramic tiles. Here is Copnor Road York Terrace here is Bapaume Road, named after the 1st World War battle site where Tanks were first used in northern France. John Webb (The Bastion) Ltd., Builders Merchants here is Military Road Southdown Motor Services Ltd., Depot In 1915 Southdown took over the Horndean Light Railway replacing the trams with motor buses, the buses running in their distinctive green and cream livery as opposed to the Corporation vehicles which were maroon and white. There were two garages in Portsmouth, Hilsea and Hyde Park Road. Buses operated for this company in East Hampshire and Sussex. The Portsmouth branch had buses that went to Fareham, 45, Droxford, 139, Waterlooville, 40/41, Havant and Hayling Island, 146/147, Alton, 38 and Petersfield. Several buses operated in the Havant area and there was a through bus to Brighton,

31. A. E. Hayter & Sons (Portchester) Ltd., Service Station Was earlier the Bastion Restaurant, then the Bastion Service Station.

Lyndhurst Road, named after New Forest town

West Side

39   Raymond Halfacre, Cycle Engineer

here is Laburnum Grove

59   F. G. Turner, Decorator

here is Wykeham Road
            Church of the Ascension, see Stubbington Avenue

here is Stubbington Avenue
            Secondary Modern School (Girls), see Crofton Road.
            Primary School (Mixed and Infants)

85   N. W. Stubbington, grocer

here is Kirby Road
East Side

here is Laburnum Grove

68   Lyndhurst Stores (W. C. Rutter & W. J. Hoole)

here is Copythorn Road

70   J. Summers, Fruiterer & Greengrocer

"Both shops later became Birds, and the shop at 68 was enlarged and that at 70 converted into housing."

here are Stubbington Avenue and Kirby Road

Madeira Road
South Side

119   National Deposit Friendly Society (Portsmouth North)

North Side

2   Mrs. K. E. Phebey, Grocer
12   Hy. Bowyer, Builder, Decorator and General House Repairs
16   Mrs. M. D. Hurst, Teacher of Music

here is Windermere Road

74   Pettit & Smith, Decorators

Mayfield Road, probably named after the Sussex Village
North Side
On 7th October 1932 the Northern Secondary School was opened by Lord Mayor Alderman F. G. Foster, with accommodation for 600 boys and 600 girls. The

architect was Adrian Sharp of the Education Committee and the builder Samuel Salter. The cost was £125,000. Later it became the Northern Grammar School and then Mayfield Comprehensive.

South Side
74   C. Carpenter, Grocer on the corner of Randolph Road

Merrivale Road Residential only

The Promenade
2-3   was the Radiant Health Centre, Michael Maybury

"Our shop called the Radiant Health Centre, was rather hidden in a walkway called The Promenade connecting Gladys Avenue to London Road. The shop was opposite a tobacconist. Soon after we opened this branch, I visited the manager of Melanie's, which was a large Co-op General Store, which had a restaurant. Very quickly we arranged for good fresh vegetarian salads to be made available to their customers, so we could send our health-minded customers there. This was a very popular move. There may still be some residents who remember Melanies Store which burnt down years later, when it was vacant. At the Radiant Health Centre, one of our regular customers was a lady who had a grown up son who had been damaged by a vaccination when he was a baby. It was very piteous to see, and we could only offer the help of basic nourishment, because of the severe damage that had left him badly disabled. On one occasion, soon after we opened our Health Food Centre, we wanted to reach the ordinary shoppers in North End, who would not normally walk north of the North End Junction. I filled our display windows with normal healthy food goods, and labelled each item with a 'lucky number'. During lunch, I closed the shop, which was quite normal in those days, and gave out leaflets, advertising the shop to shoppers walking in London Road. The unusual thing was that each leaflet had a different number, and shoppers were invited to visit the shop, and look into our display windows, seeking to find an item with a matching numbers. If they spotted their number, they only had to enter the shop and claim their free gift. We found this a very good way of introducing people to the concept of a health food store, and the items we sold. Much goodwill was created this way. In addition, to generate immediate interest, I interleaved pound notes occasionally among the leaflets, so when someone received money as well as a leaflet, they were very pleased. They would inevitably visit the shop and possibly tell friends about this crazy idea. I did not understand publicity in those days, otherwise I would have contacted the local News to let them know about this crazy stunt. They would have written a good article about our new shop. It was not till later I realised how interested a local newspaper is in the novel ideas and new businesses that open in their district. On a later occasion, I was unloading goods late at night into the shop at North End, when, who should come running down the middle of Gladys Avenue, a man chased by a policeman! I (perhaps foolishly) stood in the middle of the road with my arms spread out and the man stopped! It was only later that I realised that I never got a thank you from the policeman. Over the years attitudes to the police have unfortunately altered, but I sometimes wonder whether some of the blame rests with the police themselves with their lack of public relations expertise. Also, nowadays, all of us are reluctant to assist the police for fear of being blamed for some crime ourselves, or creating injury to a criminal, for which we would be responsible."

Mike Maybury

4   Frederick Trenaman, Tobacconist

Randolph Road, named after the Rev. Dr. Randolph, Bishop of Guildford, see Ascension Church under Stubbington Avenue.

West Side
here are Kirby, Thurbern, Mayfield, Inhurst, Hewett Roads and St Chad's and Battenburg Avenues
99   E. L. Strong, Grocer
101   Miss W. M. Barnes, Confectioner

East Side
6   Donald Perman, Builder

here is Kirby Road
46   Miss Kathleen Coleman, Teacher of Music

here is Mayfield Road
60   Smeeds Ltd., Wine Merchants. Still an off licence in 2005.

here are Inhurst Road and St Chad's and Battenburg Avenues, Compton, Madeira and Torrington Roads

St Chad's Avenue, named since there was to have been a church of that name on the corner. However, the church was built in Battenburg Avenue as St. Nicholas' Church.

North Side
1   Portsmouth Dairies Ltd.

here is Randolph Road

St Swithun's Road, named after St. Swithun of Winchester as most of the land in the area was formerly owned by Winchester College.
South Side
17   Ernest Brown, Insurance Agent

Stubbington Avenue, earlier Stubbington Lane named after the farm which was centred around the area where the Ascension Church now stands.

South Side
2   White & Co. Ltd., Furniture Removers and Storers, Offices

here are Emsworth and Drayton Roads
26   Lieut.-Col Harold Smithers, Veterinary Surgeon

here is Beresford Road
48   Portsmouth Voluntary Association for Blind Social Centre here are Balfour Road and Wykeham Avenue Church of the Ascension Started in an Iron Mission Hall in 1908. The permanent church commenced with the laying of the foundation stone on 4th October 1913. A Procession started from St Marks and proceeded to the Ascension site where the Bishop of Guildford Rev Dr. Randolph laid the foundation stone. The Procession then carried on to the site of St Saviours where the Bishop of Southampton laid the foundation stone. Funds for both churches coming from the Bishop of Winchester's six churches fund, the Bernard Wilson Church (St James) had already received some funds. The builder of both churches was S. Salter. One discordant note in the unique outdoor celebration was a silent demonstration by the Kensit Party. Along the line of the procession placards were raised over the heads of people protesting against Romanising practices, "Ritualism is a gigantic fraud" and "Shame on Romanising Bishops" were printed on some boards in bold black type. John Kensit led the party and stood for parliament at Brighton in 1900 on the Ritualistic Issue. The church could seat 800 and the architect was A. E. Cogswell.

here is Lyndhurst Road
162   Edward McIlroy & Son, Coal Merchants.

here is Kensington Road
212   Gilbert Eades, Pianoforte Tuner.

"At one time he owned a black Mayflower car"

230   Flippance & Co., Timber Merchant. Still a timber merchant in 2005.

North Side

       Portsea Island Mutual Co-operative Society Ltd., Restaurant
31   Oriel Nursing Home
       North End Bowling Club, James Chimmeck, Secretary.
       Has been derelict in recent years but is now to be updated and include housing on part of the site.

here are Beresford, Balfour and Fearon Roads
81   Harold Suter & Peter Roberts, Physician & Surgeons, Surgery

here are Randolph, Crofton, Lyndhurst, Kenyon, Chelmsford and Kensington Roads
197   Rita (Miss R. M. Gurr), Ladies' Hairdresser

Thurbern Road Residential only

Torrington Road, named after the village.
North Side
here is Windermere Road
51-55   The Phoenix Built in 1937 for Brickwoods. Portsmouth Jazz Club met here for many years.

Wallington Road, named after the village.
North Side
44-46   F. C. Dowse, Lock-up Garages

Windermere Road, named after the lake. Is not even residential.

Winton Road, named after the Sheriff of Hampshire. Residential only.

Wykeham Avenue. Residential only.

Wykeham Road
North Side
69   Miss Lily Kneller, Teacher of Music.